Bobby Jindal

The Transformational Story of a Brown-skinned,
Die-hard Conservative in the Deep South
(who will probably be your President someday)

Xander Cricket

Manufactured in the United States of America

10 9 8 7 6 5 4 3 2 1

ISBN 1442129182

EAN-13 9781442129184

To Ella

Contents

INTRODUCTION

Newt Gingrich calls him the "the most transformative young governor in America."[1] Rush Limbaugh says he's "brilliant," "the real deal,"[2] and refers to him as "the next Ronald Reagan."[3] Michelle Malkin praises him as an "extraordinary, young, dynamic, whip-smart, staunchly conservative Republican."[4] To many conservatives, he is one of the best hopes the movement has for regaining control of the Republican Party.

Bobby Jindal is the Republican governor of the state of Louisiana. He is one of the most conservative figures in American politics and, at age 37, is the country's youngest governor. He was rumored to be on John McCain's short list for vice-president in the 2008 election, and is widely regarded as a serious contender for the 2012 or 2016 Republican primaries.

Jindal's rise to power has been astonishing in its speed. He graduated Brown University with a perfect 4.0 GPA and studied political theory at Oxford as a Rhodes Scholar. Working as a type of "community organizer," he became head of Louisiana's Department of Health and

1

Hospitals when he was only 24 years-old.[5] Soon after, he moved to another key state position: president of the eight-campus public university system. He progressed to become a congressman representing the New Orleans suburbs, and in 2007 he made a bid for governor of Louisiana. Jindal won in a legitimate landslide, capturing 94% of the state's parishes.

Bobby Jindal is an embodiment of the American Dream. His parents immigrated to Louisiana from India while his mother was pregnant with him. He worked hard throughout school and never achieved less than an A. He rose to the top by performing his roles tirelessly and producing results. He has been an inspirational go-getter all of his life.

What follows is a brief introduction to a man who could one day become president of the United States. His early life and long career in politics reflect remarkable diligence and authenticity. He is a Christian wholeheartedly devoted to his Christian, conservative principles. He was won over to the Republican Party as a teenager by President Ronald Reagan and continues to advocate for Reaganesque governance. He is almost precisely what conservative Republicans were searching for in the 2007-2008 primaries but were denied. If he

2

stands firms and is able to defeat the pervasive, liberal influences on the Republican Party, Bobby Jindal is nearly certain to become the party's nominee at some point in the future.

EARLY LIFE

Piyush "Bobby" Jindal was born June 10, 1971, to a Hindu family in Baton Rouge, Louisiana. His parents emigrated from India only six months before his birth so that his mother, Raj, could pursue a graduate degree in nuclear physics at Louisiana State University.[6] Bobby's father, Amar, grew up in the village of Khanpura in the Punjab region of India,[7] and was the only one of nine siblings to attend high school.[8] He completed an engineering degree at Guru Nanak Dev University before moving to the United States.[9] Amar and Raj set exceedingly high standards for their son. He was expected to come home from school with no less than a 100% on every test.[10]

Piyush declared himself "Bobby" at age four in honor of his favorite "Brady Bunch" character. He refused to go by anything else.[11] Jindal says there was no great thought put into the name change;[12] he identified with the character "Bobby" and liked the name. He explained in an interview with CBS, "every day after school, I'd come home and I'd watch 'The Brady Bunch.'

And I identified with Bobby, you know? He was about my age, and Bobby stuck."[13]

Wendy Morgan, Jindal's fourth grade teacher, remembers him as a "very bright, but very shy" child. She tried to bring him out of his shell by casting him as the boisterous mayor in "The Pied Piper." Morgan recalls Jindal "didn't think he could do it," but "he set his mind to it and he did it."[14]

Jindal was drawn to politics by the Reagan Revolution. He was only nine years-old when the Gipper came to power. He was inspired by President Reagan's accomplishments and popularity, and although his family was loosely affiliated with the Democrats, he readily broke with them to join the party of Reagan. He recalls, "I grew up in a time when there weren't a whole lot of Republicans in [Louisiana]. But I identified with President Reagan. He was, I thought, a very successful president."[15]

Only a few years after converting to Reaganism, Jindal underwent another life-changing conversion. His evangelical friend Kent gave him a paperback Bible for Christmas when he was twelve years-old. Jindal had been raised in a "strong Hindu culture" and at the time considered himself "anti-Christian." Still, he decided not to discard the Bible, and instead hid it his closet.[16] He began discussing religion regularly with Kent and gradually warmed to the idea of Christianity. Jindal recounts the transformation in an article published in the *New Oxford Review* in 1998:

> My parents, who came from India, imparted to me a nominal Hinduism backed by a solid belief in God and His desire for man to engage in regular prayer, but I did not make progress toward a systematic religious faith until the awkward years of junior high school. In between gossiping about girls and complaining about algebra, my best friend Kent and I argued about the meaning of life. Kent's born-again Protestant view of the world contrasted with my worldly view of religion. His view of a world motivated by love and self-sacrifice was certainly more hopeful, though to me less relevant, than my own notion of selfish actors attempting to satisfy their own desires and showing little concern for others. Kent gave me few convincing answers, but he did raise questions that were to lead me to some very surprising places. He planted the seeds.
>
> I was challenged more by the novelty of Kent's approach than by its substance, and I spent some effort trying to learn more about how my Hindu faith responded to his questions. It took my grandfather's death, at the end of my sophomore

year of high school, to concentrate my efforts. Pitaji was my idol, a successful banker who had it all, and I almost could not believe that his wealth could not save him from his mortality. Kent's questions took on more than academic importance as I pondered, for the first time, the afterlife. My grandfather was, by all accounts, a good man, but I had no assurance that he, or I, deserved entrance into heaven, if such a place existed; not even my hero's life accomplishments seemed an adequate offering. I imagined Pitaji bargaining with God, trying to offer a part of his fortune for eternal life.

What began as a search partly motivated by fear of judgment and selfish desire for assurance soon led me to appreciate at least some part of Kent's worldview. I made the startling discovery that love, not money, makes the world go round. I finally began to understand that my grandfather meant so much to me because of his love and generosity, not the expensive gifts that he used to express those feelings, and that these same traits were his life's true accomplishments. I discovered this capacity for self-sacrifice, other-consciousness, and love...[17]

Kent had made progress with Jindal, but it would take the motivation of a crush named Kathy to convince him to retrieve the Bible from his closet. He read it from cover to cover. While watching a Passion film at Kent's church,

7

Jindal was convicted of his sinfulness and "need for a savior."[18] The son of Hindu immigrants had become a Christian.

Jindal was fervent about his new faith. He studied the Bible "by flashlight" and "learned bits of Latin, Greek and Hebrew."[19] He felt compelled to hide his Christianity from his parents: "I was probably the first teenager who ever told his parents he was going to a party so that he could sneak off to church."[20] As college approached, he feared his disapproving parents would not support him financially. He wrote in a July 1994 article, "I had decided the freedom to worship Christ was more important than the material comforts provided by my parents, including the privilege to attend Brown that fall. I even made plans to attend a local university and had arranged housing as well as a job to support myself." His parents did not go so far as to cut him off, but it took years for them to accept his religion. Jindal says eventually "they realized I had not joined a bizarre cult, and instead they appreciated the new honesty in my life."[21]

His soul searching ultimately led him to conclude Protestantism lacked "scriptural cogency." He became a devoted Catholic in 1991.[22] Jindal published fifteen essays in the *New Oxford Review* and other Catholic journals between 1991 and 1998,[23] including one titled "How Catholicism Is Different: The Catholic Church Isn't Just Another Denomination."[24]

Jindal's faith is deep and authentic. A few critics have suggested his conversion was solely for political purposes. Hindu activist Ramesh Rao says "Jindal knew well that [conversion] was the only way, as an Indian-American Hindu, he could achieve his political ambitions."[25] However, the evidence is strongly against such a claim. Jindal's Christianity put him at odds with his Hindu family, and his particularly Catholic faith has often been a political liability. His no-abortion-under-any-circumstance belief dissuades many voters, and in his 2007 gubernatorial election, Louisiana Democrats played off the Protestant-Catholic divide to cast Jindal as a bigoted anti-Protestant.[26] Jindal quips, "If I wanted the aesthetics without the inconvenient morality, I could become Episcopalian."[27]

Amidst shaping his Christian, conservative beliefs, Jindal also excelled as a student at Baton Rouge Magnet High School. His principal remembers young Jindal as the "epitome of an academic student… He had success written all over him."[28] Jindal was active in numerous academic groups. At age 14, he won awards in language and photography at the convention of the Louisiana Junior Classical League, an organization for students of Latin, Greek, and the classics.[29] The following year, he won third place in math against 630 other students at Xavier University's Math-Science Olympiad.[30] He competed with the Baton Rouge Magnet Quiz Bowl team and, at another contest, won first place in math.[31] Jindal was the grand prize winner in the economics division of the 1987 state fair with his project titled "Foreign Invasion of Corporate America."[32] As a reward, he was given a luncheon tour of the New Orleans branch of the Federal Reserve Bank of Atlanta.[33]

Jindal also was active in several clubs. As a senior, he was president of the Junior Academy of Science; vice-president of Mu Alpha Theta (a mathematics honor society) and Beta Club (a service organization); and treasurer of Interact (another service club) and his Explorer Post (a subsidiary of Boy Scouts). Through Interact and the Beta Club, Jindal worked with the Salvation Army, Muscular Dystrophy Association and other charities to raise money for their projects. He also volunteered with the Arts and Humanities Council. For his community service and academic performance, Jindal was the 1988 Baton Rouge recipient of Wal-Mart's Foundation Community Scholarship.[34]

Jindal graduated high school in 1988 with a 4.62 grade point average. He entered Brown University in the fall with a double major in biology and public policy.[35] He faltered at first, nearly failing his first test,[36] but remained as diligent as ever and ultimately achieved A's in all his courses. He graduated Brown with a perfect 4.0 GPA.[37]

Arshad Ahsanuddin, a close friend from college, told *Newsweek* that Jindal often sported penny loafers with actual pennies in them around campus. Jindal claimed "it was the traditional way to wear that type of shoe." When a professor asked the hypothetical question "If a high school only took the brightest students, would it be mostly white or mostly black?" Jindal passed Ahsanuddin a note that jokingly said "all Asian."[38]

Jindal studied biology because his parents were determined he would become a medical doctor.[39] Although he completed his med school preparation impeccably, he continued to be intrigued by politics. He interned for U.S. Representatives Bob Livingston and Jim McCrery of Louisiana while still a student. McCrery was impressed by a giant manuscript Jindal wrote on Medicare reform.[40] When graduation came, Jindal had two safe options that would delight any parent: Harvard Medical School or Yale Law School. He declined both offers, instead accepting a Rhodes scholarship to study theoretical politics at Oxford. His parents were nonetheless delighted. The Baton Rouge *Advocate* reported in spring of 1992:

> Amar and Raj Jindal hosted a party at Ashley Manor March 27 to honor their son, Piyush "Bobby" Jindal, who graduated in three and one-half years from Brown University with a perfect 4.0 average. He is one of only five Louisianians ever to receive a Rhodes Scholarship and will study for the next two years at Oxford University in England. He won a place on the All-USA First Academic Team sponsored by USA Today and has already been accepted at Harvard Medical School when he returns from England. Family members flew in from Canada and Detroit for the event, which was also attended by the honoree's college friends from around the country.[41]

After returning from London, Jindal embarked on a well-paid stint as a consultant at McKinsey and Company in Washington, D.C.[42] His projects at the firm included advising CEO's on a health care information technology venture.[43] Looking back on the position later

12

in life, Jindal said "It was a great place to learn how large organizations make decisions… It was a great education in the business world."[44]

Jindal soon turned his sights back to Louisiana. He went home to the Bayou State in 1995 because, he said in an interview, "I think the quality of life is high here, and I like the sense of community."[45] He went to Representative McCrery and asked to be recommended for the job of Louisiana health secretary. McCrery asked if Jindal, then 24, would settle for "deputy secretary." Jindal said no. McCrery got him the interview with Governor Mike Foster. The governor was pleasantly surprised by his young applicant, and in January, 1996, Jindal was appointed Secretary of the Department of Health and Hospitals.[46] His career in politics had begun.

BAYOU BUREAUCRAT

At the young age of 24, Jindal was confronted with colossal problems as head of Louisiana's biggest bureaucracy, the Department of Health and Hospitals.[47] He was in charge of 13,000 employees and a $3.9 billion budget.[48] The department was in financial trouble and would require a serious overhaul if it were to operate efficiently. Governor Mike Foster placed full confidence in his "genius" appointment: "I am not a gambler. I am a very conservative person... And, I am very, very comfortable that this is not a gamble... This man is going to go into that department and engender a lot of respect."[49] A few months later, after Jindal was off to a good start, the governor admitted Jindal was a bit of a "gamble," but said he had not wanted "anyone well entrenched in the health care system" – a system which desperately needed to be cleaned up.[50] Jindal's youthful idealism and energy would be great assets on the job.

Jindal was determined to weed out those who were taking advantage of the state. As with any large bureaucracy, the state health care system provided ample opportunity for corrupt deals and "lost" money. When Jindal took the reins, he said "there is only one group of people who should be scared... Those are people who are cheating the system today, because there is not going to be any more tolerance for that kind of abuse and fraud." He vowed to "change the system so we don't reward such people."[51] Jindal acknowledged the task would not be easy: "It's an agency that's grown too quickly and is now broke... It can't be fixed overnight."[52]

One of his first efforts was to recoup $26.7 million in overpayments to private psychiatric hospitals.[53] He then compelled nursing homes to follow state regulations by threatening to deny them new Medicaid admissions. Unlike the previous DHH administrator, Jindal made receipt of Medicaid funds contingent upon compliance with regulations. He was immediately applauded by the American Association of Retired Persons, Citizens for Quality Nursing Home Care, and the Louisiana Health Care Campaign, among other groups.[54]

Jindal reworked the state's standards for healthcare such that they matched private sector standards. Louisiana had previously provided inpatient, 30-day substance abuse programs, in contrast to the 14-day inpatient programs available in the private sector.

Jindal cut the state's program to 20 days. The department predicted 1,962 more people would be served each year as a result of the change.[55]

Jindal also tried to implement more pay-for-use measures, attaching small fees to state health services. He said of his plan, "A $1 or $2 per service payment is not going to give a disincentive to use necessary services... But some nominal payment may decrease over-utilization by those who don't really need the service. It encourages the responsible use of public resources."[56] The plan would have applied basic economic principles to the state's health care system. The senate nixed his idea.[57]

Louisiana's pharmacy program was rapidly becoming untenable when Jindal took over DHH. He capped the number of prescriptions adult Medicaid clients could receive at five per month. This figure still placed Louisiana at the high end of state benefits, with most capping prescriptions at three to five per month. Jindal justified the move by noting Louisiana spent about $100 more per Medicaid recipient on prescription drugs than other southern states.[58]

While tackling the problems of Louisiana health care, Jindal also made advances in his love life. He reconnected with his first crush from school, a girl of

Indian descent named Supriya Jolly. The two never had any classes together because Supriya was a year younger, but Jindal had admired her from a distance: "She was the most beautiful girl I'd ever seen." He called her after another date cancelled on him and took her to a Mardi Gras ball. According to Jindal they had an "amazing" time.[59] He recalls, "We quickly fell in love and realized that we wanted to spend our lives together."[60] The couple was married at St. Joseph's Cathedral of Baton Rouge in 1997.[61]

Supriya is said to rival her husband in brains. She has a degree in chemical engineering and an MBA from Tulane University. At the time she and Jindal began dating, Supriya was working for Monsanto Chemicals at a unit that produced the herbicide Roundup. The job required her to wear a hard hat and steel-toed boots. She said in an interview with the Baton Rouge *Advocate,* "I think Bobby got a kick out of seeing me when he met me at work for one of our first dates." She later contributed to Albermarle Corp. in marketing, business strategy, and research and development, and also completed the coursework of a doctoral degree in business from LSU.[62]

With a wife by his side, Jindal contemplated leaving DHH for a different role. He was hailed by *The*

Advocate as having "brought Louisiana's runaway Medicaid program under control." He cut the DHH budget by $1 billion and achieved two-year departmental surpluses of $200 million. He was renowned for his zero tolerance policy on fraud, having recouped $28 million from doctors, hospitals, and other providers who abused the Medicaid program.[63] Brown University listed the following accomplishments' of its young alumnus:

- Reducing the Department of Health and Hospital's full-time work force by 1,000 employees while maintaining services;

- Increasing immunization rates for two-year-olds who visited health units from 55 percent five years ago to 80 percent [in 1998];

- Reducing by one-half the tobacco sales to minors, moving Louisiana three years ahead of the national schedule for tobacco sales cuts;

- Reducing per-person spending in Medicaid from a high of $3,452 in 1995 to $3,127 [in 1998].[64]

It was time for Jindal's next challenge. In January of 1998, he accepted a six-figure job as executive director of the National Bipartisan Commission on the Future of Medicare. U.S. Representative Bill Thomas of California said Jindal had "rescued Medicaid" in Louisiana, "and now the United States needs him to help rescue Medicare."[65] In his capacity, Jindal directed the 17-member staff of the Commission, a group of legislators charged with evaluating and making recommendations to strengthen the Medicare program in time for the retirement of Baby Boomers.[66]

The Commission's final report was issued on March 16, 1999. Its primary recommendation was that Medicare be changed to a market-based Premium Support model.[67] Jindal said the plan alone would not save Medicare, but would "put it on a better track" and make it sustainable until at least 2020.[68] Although the proposal received bipartisan support, President Clinton defeated it by gathering no votes in Congress.[69]

At the conclusion of the Commission, Jindal returned to Louisiana uncertain if he would stay in public service or transition to the private sector.[70] He briefly researched how Louisiana could get the most return from its portion of the $4.4 billion national tobacco settlement.[71] Then, in April of 1999, Jindal received another significant post in Governor Mike Foster's government: president of Louisiana's eight-campus university system.[72]

Some questioned why Jindal, a non-educator who lacked a terminal degree, would be placed at the head of the system, but Foster once again expressed full confidence in his appointment. Regardless of Jindal's inexperience in education, Louisianans had seen him reform their health care system and were, by and large, glad to have him back.[73] Paul Koenig, professor emeritus at LSU, wrote:

> Several commentators have decried Gov. Mike Foster's decision to nominate Bobby Jindal as president of the University of Louisiana system. The objectors suppose that Mr. Jindal is less than properly qualified to hold such a post. I would respectfully disagree.
>
> As a longtime university faculty member and administrator, I have seen no evidence that the president of a university system must himself have risen through the faculty ranks, or hold an advanced degree.
>
> He must, of course, be intelligent, energetic and personable, and a capable manager, and Mr. Jindal gives every indication of possessing those traits and abilities.[74]

Jindal began his appointment by touring the eight campuses of the university system. Soon after, he devised

a nine-point plan for improving the academic centers.[75]
The Baton Rouge *Advocate* reported "The bureaucratic
tornado known as Bobby Jindal apparently has struck
with full force at the offices of the University of
Louisiana System. Weeks after becoming president of the
system, Jindal already has produced a slew of new policy
drafts, three areas of bureaucratic concentration and nine
strategic initiatives." His first three proposals were to
allow each campus to manage its day-to-day affairs; to
standardize the rules to be uniform for all campuses; and
to develop objective performance indicators for
measuring college presidents. The *Advocate* gave his
plan a positive review, asserting "It is almost needless to
say that this is a good idea." The story called Jindal's
plan "right out of the playbook utilized by business
consultants."[76]

Jindal emphasized research at the universities by
establishing a research and development office at every
campus. He offered rewards to universities and faculties
for groundbreaking research and made it easier for
students and faculty to commercialize their inventions.
He also met with local business groups to encourage them
to partner with the universities on sponsored research
projects.[77] Johnson & Johnson teamed up with schools for

biological research, Computer Associates developed relationships with computer science departments, and the National Association of Manufacturers partnered with regional schools in offering new courses to its employees electronically.[78]

Jindal also attempted to establish better relationships between the university faculty members and K-12 public schools. Professors were sent into public schools to spend a college quarter teaching classes. The idea was to give them hands-on experience of the challenges faced by K-12 teachers, and also to help the local schools by involving them in the latest research and technology.[79]

The Shreveport *Times* reported in January of 2001 that Jindal's efforts were paying off. The USL system's research and grant funding rose 10% in 2000. Grambling State University's mathematics/computer science department was awarded $9.4 million by the U.S. army to develop human resource software. Louisiana Tech won extended funding for research in micro-manufacturing, applied physics and trenchless technology. Northwestern State University secured contracts for work force development. The paper affirmed, "Jindal is right when he says such research boosts economic development in Louisiana."[80]

Two months later, another big change came in Jindal's career. President Bush nominated him to be assistant secretary for planning and evaluation at the federal Department of Health and Human Services. Jindal readily accepted the position.

Louisianans were sad to see the whiz kid go. Jindal's term as president of the university system saw improved graduation and student retention rates, as well as a rise in admissions standards.[81] Louisiana Tech President Dan Reneau said "our loss is the nation's gain… Bobby's done a great job. It will be a loss to the educational system."[82]

The Medicare appointment gave Jindal valuable experience in federal government. It was an excellent opportunity, returning him to the health care industry in which he had already succeeded so admirably and giving him an up-close look at a president's administration. It wasn't long, however, before he was ready to quit his post and go home to Louisiana. In January of 2003, rumors began growing in Louisiana that the wunderkind might come back to run for governor.

The rumors proved true. On February 26, 2003, Jindal returned to the Bayou State and, with Governor Mike Foster and Christian Coalition leader Billy McCormack at his side, announced he was running for governor.[83]

AN AMBITIOUS BID

Jindal faced competition from five Democrats and eleven Republicans.[84] His ethnicity and young age of 31 were immediately cited as liabilities. Jindal replied "Louisianans are better than that. They will select the best candidate."[85]

Jindal outlined three priorities for improving the state. First, he would ensure Louisiana was a place businesses could survive by cutting taxes. Second, he would focus on Louisiana's assets – "we can't be all things to all people." Third, he would bring the public more into government operations.[86]

Jindal spoke frequently on job creation. He set out to stop the state's "brain drain," devising ways to keep graduates of Louisiana schools in the state.[87] He denounced the business taxes punishing companies and emphasized the importance of technical and community colleges in training the workforce.[88] He said jobs would be created by reducing corporate tax rates, streamlining permit processes, educating the work force, and reforming the civil court system.[89]

Economic initiatives were Jindal's top priority. He appealed to the business community by promising less government interference, less cumbersome regulation, and fewer taxes. He announced he would "oppose and veto any and all efforts to increase taxes."[90] Always a fan of lists, Jindal summarized his agenda in various multi-point plans. His economic development initiatives were unveiled in the form of an 18-point plan, which included efforts to oppose oil and gas taxes and to provide focused incentives to the state's industries.[91]

Jindal's goals for strengthening faith and values in the state were presented in a 16-point plan. The measures included aggressive promotion of adoption as an alternative to abortion, educational programs to combat divorce, and faith-based solutions to social problems. Jindal also vowed to oppose the expansion of gambling in the state and to fight the "radical gun control lobby." He said "our government should reflect our values and should embrace the great work of the faith community."[92] On the education front, Jindal advocated a school voucher program whereby students at failing schools could attend private or charter schools.[93]

George W. Bush still enjoyed high approval ratings in 2003 and was an asset for candidate Jindal.

Bush remained the icon of "compassionate conservatism," a Christian leader with known values to which people could relate. When speaking to the Capital City Kiwanis Club, Jindal reminded the group that he had worked for Bush and knew him personally.[94] Jindal told another group that if elected, his first call would be to George W. Bush to discuss restoring Louisiana's coastline.[95]

Jindal cast himself as the change candidate, the individual free of corruption and capable of a clean administration. A resident of West Monroe gave Jindal the following endorsement in the Monroe *News-Star*:

> It's time for change. In the governor's race this year, we have a lot of candidates to choose from. It seems to me that there are a lot of candidates who offer "more of the same."
>
> Bobby Jindal, who is a former Bush administration official, is the only candidate who offers a clear vision. We have done a good job in providing education to Louisiana students, but we have failed at creating jobs. Jindal has a clear vision for economic development in Louisiana. One can imagine why businesses wouldn't want to move here. They are tired of politics as usual and corruption. Jindal is the only candidate without a history of corruption and controversy.[96]

One of the more humorous stunts of the campaign was a snub to French President Jacques Chirac. Jindal denounced Chirac for not standing "shoulder-to-shoulder" with the U.S. on the war in Iraq. He called for the uninviting of Chirac to the closing ceremonies of the Louisiana Purchase Bicentennial Celebration in December, 2003.[97] He was the first candidate to withdraw the invitation.[98]

When the primaries arrived on October 4, Jindal easily won with 33% of the vote.[99] Many were optimistic he could pull off a win in the runoff election, but he would nonetheless have a daunting, month-long battle ahead of him against his opponent, Democrat Kathleen Blanco.

Mud flew as the election heated up. Democrat Buddy Leach called Jindal a "career politician" who would let Big Oil and Big Gas run the state.[100] U.S. Senator John Breaux said Jindal was not executive material. He diminished him as a mere "staff person" who "did what other people told him to do."[101] Ashley Bell, an LSU law student and national head of the College Democrats, caused uproar when he incorrectly identified Jindal as an "Arab-American" in an e-mail to fellow College Democrats. The state Democratic Party

28

immediately threw Bell under the bus, issuing a statement that "Bell's deplorable remarks should not deter the focus of this election."[102] The "deplorable remark" was nothing more than calling Jindal an Arab-American, but it nonetheless put Democrats on edge.

Jindal and Blanco differed very little on social issues. Both supported the death penalty.[103] Both opposed legislation protecting gays and lesbians against discrimination. Both were highly rated by the NRA. Both opposed abortion, though to slightly different degrees. Blanco advocated for exceptions in the cases of rape, incest, or to save the life of the mother; Jindal would not allow abortion under any circumstance. He said he followed the Catholic Church's teaching on the matter: "The church doesn't teach abortion's OK to save the life of the mother. The church does teach that there are procedures to save the life of the mother that may have the unintended consequence [of] the loss of the life of the fetus. But that wouldn't be an abortion, so that would be OK."[104]

Running as a Republican, Jindal was uncharacteristically able to win over more than a few black voters. New Orleans' BOLD, the Black Organization for Leadership Development, endorsed

Jindal for his record on education and health care. Doug
Evans, president of BOLD, said "Bobby is more
conservative than most candidates BOLD endorses...
Nonetheless, his record on health care and education
proves beyond a shadow of a doubt he has a big heart for
all Louisianians – and don't let anyone else tell you
otherwise."[105]

As election day approached, it appeared the 32
year-old Jindal just might defeat his 60 year-old
opponent. Four days before voting, Jindal held a 10-point
lead. The young candidate and his crew were confident
he would soon be in office. Blanco launched a series of
last-minute attack ads criticizing his no-exception stance
on abortion. The ads went unanswered, effectively
obliterating Jindal's lead. On Saturday, November 15,
Louisianans cast their ballots. Jindal lost with 48% of the
vote.[106]

Political scientists blamed Jindal's
"overconfidence" and apparent "intolerance" in the
debates. Governor Mike Foster blamed his protégé's
strategists, saying "they broke the cardinal rule: you
cannot allow anyone to attack you without answering
it."[107] U.S. Representative Bob Livingston agreed:
"When somebody goes on an attack, you've got to

respond to it."[108] Murphy Foster, the governor's son, said there "was a barrage of negative ads after she pledged she wouldn't. He did not fire back. He's a man of his word. He said he wouldn't do it." Jindal defended his strategy of not returning the attacks, saying "from the first day of this campaign, I felt my job was to tell people why they should vote for me, not why they shouldn't vote for my opponent."[109]

Jindal's loss was, in some ways, a blessing. He had more time to gain experience and enjoy his family before assuming the pressures of governorship. By the time of the election, Jindal and wife Supriya had a daughter, Selia, and son, Shaan. Jindal's loss also allowed him to avoid the catastrophe of Hurricane Katrina. When the hurricane hit and Blanco was ill-prepared, her prospects for reelection were ruined. Jindal was instead able to address Katrina as a legislator without any liability.

After losing to Blanco, Jindal quickly re-grouped and organized a campaign for the U.S. House of Representatives. In November of 2004, he was elected to represent Louisiana's First Congressional District. For the fourth time in his life, he was going to work in Washington, this time as Congressman Bobby Jindal.

CONGRESSMAN JINDAL

Jindal was elected to represent Louisiana's First
Congressional District. At the time, the district was
comprised of the western suburbs of New Orleans and the
parishes north of Lake Pontchartrain. He won easily with
78% of the vote,[110] making him the second Indian-
American elected to Congress.[111] Jindal was selected by
his colleagues to lead the 2004 class of House Republican
freshmen. He also was appointed by House Majority
Whip Roy Blount to serve as assistant whip, a position
which entails rounding up votes to pass legislation.
Prominent conservatives immediately took notice of
Jindal. Fred Barnes, executive editor of *The Weekly
Standard*, wrote "Jindal is destined to be a star in
Washington."[112]

Jindal won on a 5-point platform: ensuring the
safety of Americans in the war on terror; reducing the cost
of health care; shrinking the national debt; coming up
with funding and solutions for coastal erosion; and
supporting programs that would "solidify families."[113] He
served on three committees while in the House –

Education and the Workforce, Homeland Security, and Resources – and was elected to two terms.

Jindal's voting record in Congress was, for the most part, consistent with his stated, conservative agenda. A full record of his votes is available through the Library of Congress.[114]

Jindal was thoroughly pro-life. He voted yes on the Abortion Pain Bill (HR 6099), which ensured women seeking an abortion would be fully informed of the pain experienced by their unborn child. He supported the Child Interstate Abortion Notification Act (S 403), criminalizing the transportation of minors across state lines to obtain an abortion. He voted against the Overseas Military Facilities Abortion Amendment (H AMDT 209), which would have allowed privately funded abortions at U.S. military facilities overseas. He voted against the Stem Cell Research Bill of 2005 (HR 810) authorizing the use of human embryonic stem cells.

Jindal was steadfastly conservative on other social issues as well. He supported the Same-Sex Marriage Resolution (H J Res 88) that would have amended the Constitution to define marriage as between one man and one woman. He voted yes on a bill extending abstinence education.[115] He supported the Trigger Lock Amendment

(H AMDT 1156), a measure that prevented funding for enforcement of a law requiring guns be sold with locks on them. He voted yes on the Internet Gambling Bill (HR 4411) prohibiting Internet gambling. He voted no on the Medical Marijuana Use Amendment (H AMDT 272), which would have allowed states to authorize the use of medical marijuana. One of the only potential aberrations on Jindal's conservative record was a "no" vote on the Human Cloning Prohibition Act of 2007, which would have banned human cloning (defined as the implantation of a cloned egg into a uterus).

On healthcare, Jindal voted against the reauthorization and expansion of the State Children's Health Insurance Program (HR 3162), but later supported a different version of the legislation while campaigning for governor.[116] He voted no on the Prescription Drug Imports amendment (H AMDT 734) prohibiting the importation of prescription drugs by consumers. He voted yes to a budget resolution (H Res 653) ensuring hospitals could not deny treatment to Medicaid patients who were unable to provide their co-pay for non-emergency situations. He supported the Malpractice Liability Reform Bill (HR 5), which placed numerous restrictions on medical malpractice lawsuits. He voted yes to the Cheeseburger Bill (HR 554), prohibiting lawsuits against anyone in the food industry on claims that the plaintiff's food caused obesity or weight gain.

Jindal mainly stayed to the right on environmental issues. He voted no on the Energy Act of 2007 (HR 6), an invasive bill that, among other things, denied a deduction for income attributable to domestic production of oil and natural gas. He voted against the Endangered Species Amendment (H AMDT 588), which broadened the range of the original Endangered Species Act. He approved the Horse Slaughter Prohibition bill (HR 503), establishing a pilot program to decide if the killing of equines for human consumption should be banned nationwide. He supported the Deep Ocean Energy Resources Act of 2006 (HR 4761), permanently banning oil and natural gas drilling within 50 miles of the states' shore while opening the outer continental shelf for exploration. He voted in favor of the Gasoline for America's Security Act of 2005 (HR 3893) providing for construction of new oil refineries on federal land.

Jindal's economic votes indicate a free market sentiment with an inclination toward economic meddling. He favored lower taxes, but also a number of economic regulations. He approved the Pay-As-You-Go Rule (H

35

Res 6), requiring that any tax cuts be offset by a spending cut or tax increase. He voted yes for the Death/Estate Tax and Minimum Wage Bill (HR 5970), which raised the federal minimum wage to $7.25 and increased exemptions for the Death Tax. He supported the Tax Relief Extension Reconciliation Act of 2005 (HR 4297) extending $69.96 billion in tax cuts through 2010. He approved of a free trade agreement with Oman in the U.S.-Oman Free Trade Agreement Implementation (HR 5684), but opposed CAFTA (HR 3045). He voted against a bill that would have withdrawn the U.S. from the World Trade Organization.[117] He opposed Big Labor's Union Organization Bill (HR 800).

Jindal was generally in line with the Bush Administration on national security. He voted in favor of a resolution on the Global War on Terror (H Res 861) stating the U.S. would not set an arbitrary timetable for troop withdrawal. He voted against the Guantanamo Transfer Plan (H AMDT 197) that effectively would have closed the prison at Guantanamo Bay. He opposed a resolution disapproving of President Bush's surge in Iraq.[118] He supported the Ban on Permanent Bases in Iraq (HR 2929), limiting the funding for any permanent military establishment in Iraq.

The drab legislation aside, Jindal's most exciting moment as a congressman came in the summer of 2006. Supriya was pregnant with their third child and went into labor in the middle of the night. Without time to get to a hospital, Jindal was forced to deliver the baby at home. The birth was a success and Slade Ryan Jindal entered the world a healthy baby. Looking back on the event, Supriya told CBS "It's something that I never want to experience again. He did an incredible job. But, I'm the kind of person that likes to be in the hospital with medicine."[119]

When Hurricane Katrina hit in the summer of 2005, Jindal was critical of the state and federal governments' inadequate responses.[120] He quipped that the Royal Canadian Mounted Police arrived in Washington Parish before FEMA did.[121] His district was hit hard, with his three offices in Metairie, Mandeville and Hammond all having to be closed.[122] Fortunately for Jindal, the disaster was on Kathleen Blanco's shoulders, not his. He moved legislation as he saw necessary to try to alleviate Louisianans' pain, introducing bills in Congress to help college students affected by the storm and to reimburse private hospitals providing relief.[123]

37

Jindal was dismayed by the red tape people encountered as they tried to collect from insurance. He told reporters: "I'm not particularly interested in assigning blame. What I want to ensure is whether next time we can promise people it will be better, and we can promise that all the red tape is being cut. We can't allow red tape to continually strangle the recovery effort or reconstruction."[124] In an attempt to free people from governmental burdens, Jindal introduced legislation to temporarily eliminate the federal income tax for hurricane victims.[125]

Jindal was widely appreciated for his response to Katrina. Sheriff Jack A. Stevens of St. Bernard Parish wrote the following letter to the editor thanking Jindal for his handling of the situation:

> As sheriff of St. Bernard Parish and a lifelong Democrat, I feel compelled to respond to a letter to the editor regarding Congressman Bobby Jindal.
>
> Of more than 26,000 homes in St. Bernard, very few were spared flooding when Hurricane Katrina came ashore. More than 100 people lost their lives and the toll in human suffering cannot be measured.

The 392 employees of the sheriff's department lost everything they had. The 136 vehicles owned by the department were lost, as well as most tactical equipment.

In the dark days following the hurricane, we wondered if help would ever arrive. One of the first officials to come to our aid was Rep. Jindal. He and members of his staff offered help.

It is important to note that St. Bernard is not a part of the Congressman's district; in fact, a majority of the parish voters are Democrats.

As a result of the congressman's efforts, we were successful in securing FEMA assistance replacing our fleet and equipment necessary to do our job.

On behalf of the people of St. Bernard Parish and my deputies, I would like to thank Rep. Jindal and his staff for their efforts.[126]

Democratic Governor Kathleen Blanco, on the other hand, did not fare so well in the public eye. The breakdown in coordination with FEMA was obvious. A resident of Alexandria wrote, "I wonder if Bobby Jindal had been elected governor, would he have had a squabble with the federal government?"[127] The buyer's remorse was not isolated, and talk soon began to spread of the possibility that Louisiana's whiz kid might come home from Washington to lead the state.

On November 8, 2006, the day after winning re-election to Congress, Jindal acknowledged he was looking at the approaching governor's race.[128] On January 23, 2007, the Baton Rouge *Advocate* made it official. Bobby Jindal wanted a rematch against Kathleen Blanco.[129]

THE YOUNG GOVERNOR

Jindal centered his 2007 campaign on ethics
reform. Louisiana had been brutalized by bureaucracy,
corruption, and incompetent governance in the aftermath
of Hurricane Katrina. Jindal once again presented himself
as the "change" candidate. As he revved up his campaign
efforts in July, he told a crowd in Alexandria, "We need
to declare war on corruption. We need to declare war on
incompetence. We need to declare war on excess
spending."[130] Jindal developed a 25-point plan for
cleaning up Louisianan government. Among his points
were promises to eliminate slush funds, curb wasteful
spending, and make legislators more accountable to the
public.[131]

Jindal also unveiled a 24-point plan for the
economy. He said he would eliminate several taxes on
businesses and streamline the regulatory process. He also
advocated giving better incentives to corporations to
partner with the state's universities on research. Jindal
said the top priority for improving the economy would be

ethics reform: "We can't reform our economy until we clean up our act. We've got to end corruption."[132]

The election was left wide open for Jindal when Governor Kathleen Blanco announced on March 20 – seven months before voters went to the polls – that she would not seek re-election.[133] Democrats were without a candidate and had very little time left to organize a campaign. Jindal had broad name recognition and was still very popular with the public. Eventually Democrat Walter Boasso and Independent John Georges became prominent candidates in the race, but Jindal remained the frontrunner.

As in the 2003 campaign, Jindal faced relentless attack ads from his opponents. While the previous election's ads focused on his religious stance on abortion, the 2007 ads portrayed him as an anti-Protestant, bigoted Catholic by taking his former writings on Catholicism out of context. Voters didn't fall for the smear a second time. They were outraged by the Democrats' attacks. One voter wrote, "I knew politics in Louisiana were dirty, but this last ad against Bobby Jindal has got me fighting mad."[134] Another said the "low life attack ads make me support Bobby Jindal more than ever."[135]

On October 20, 2007, 2.8 million Louisianans turned out to vote. They had eleven candidates to choose from in the open primary for governor. Jindal needed 50% of the vote to avoid another runoff election. As the results were tallied, they quickly confirmed what most analysts had expected: Bobby Jindal was the next governor of Louisiana. He won with 54% of the vote, carrying 60 of the state's 64 parishes. A review of the results showed Jindal capturing 63% of the white vote and 10% of the black vote.[136] His victory made him the youngest governor in the country, as well as the first Indian-American governor in U.S. history. He declared in his acceptance speech, "Change is not just on the way. Change begins tonight."[137]

Jindal's relatives in India celebrated at the news of his victory. Locals of his ancestral village of Khanpura distributed candy and performed a *bhangra* folk dance. His 37 year-old cousin Gulshan Jindal of Malerkotla said in an interview with the *Times of India*, "We are really proud that Bobby has finally made it and won the Governor's race. It's a great honour not just for our family, but Punjab and the nation as well as the son of this soil [has] achieved something really big."[138]

43

Jindal was sworn into office on January 14, 2008. He hit the ground running with his plans for reform. On day one, he froze all state government hiring.[139] He argued Louisiana could no longer be seen as a corrupt state, or else businesses would never operate there. A special legislative session was called to push through Jindal's ethics legislation.[140]

Only a few weeks after taking office, Jindal fulfilled his premiere pledge. The ethics reform passed in late February of 2008. The legislation was extensive: it placed strict requirements on lobbyists, required financial disclosure from elected and appointed officials in state and local government, and prohibited state officials from contracting with the state.[141] Jindal hailed the ethics package as the starting point for cleaning up the state. He reveled in a news conference:

> This is a great, historic day for Louisiana. But it's just the first step in creating a new Louisiana... We had to be ambitious and aggressive to restore the people's trust in government. We're not just going from 50th to 49th. I guarantee we'll be in at least the top five states in the country (in ethics). No other state has come this far this quickly.[142]

Jindal released his first budget soon after the reform. It included pay raises for teachers and tax cuts for businesses. Some of the highlights were:

- $307.1 million for an economic development fund to attract large projects such as an automotive plant.

- $169 million to reduce the waiting list for community-based health-care services for the disabled.

- $110 million in tax breaks to give businesses relief on utilities, corporate debt and machinery purchases.

- $70.1 million to keep teacher pay across the state at the Southern regional average, giving teachers a $1,019 annual pay raise.

- At least $65.1 million for work-force development programs.

- An additional $60 million for nursing homes.

- $3 million for research at the Pennington Biomedical Research Center.[143]

When the state had $1 billion in surplus funds to spend from the boom in oil prices, Jindal directed the funds to promoting a business friendly environment. His proposed use of the funds included:

- A one-cent decrease in the sales tax businesses paid for electricity and natural gas.

- Phase-outs of business taxes on manufacturing machinery purchases and debt.

- 50% tax deduction for up to $5,000 in private school tuition and home-schooling expenses parents pay per child.

- Exempting the federal rebate checks from being treated as taxable income.

- A move toward using the sales tax revenue from car and truck sales to pay for work on roads and highways.

- Using about half of the $1.1 billion state government surplus to improve roads, bridges and ports.[144]

Jindal's first 100 days were widely regarded as a success. The Monroe *News-Star* declared "through two special legislative sessions and part of a regular session, the Republican wonder boy has steamrolled his agenda through a Legislature ready and willing to either help him or get out of his way." State Senator Bob Kostelka said "I think he's accomplished more in three months than any other administration in history." Former Governor Mike Foster also approved, saying "He's absolutely met my expectations; he's a perpetual motion machine... Look how long people have been trying to do something on ethics and reduce business taxes."[145] The *News-Star* summarized Jindal's initial accomplishments as follows:

> He put everyone to work on day one with two special legislative sessions and now a regular session. He's delivered on ethics reform and tax reform to improve Louisiana's business climate. He's working now to revamp work-force development. And he has spread the wealth of a budget surplus... Yes, it's only 100 days. But Louisiana's governor already has proved what can happen when people work together to achieve a goal.[146]

Jindal was not entirely a free marketeer in his first year as governor. The state legislature briefly discussed eliminating Louisiana's personal income tax. Unsure of how the elimination would work in the state budget, Jindal's administration intervened and proposed a lesser tax cut package instead.[147] In May of 2008, Jindal proposed increasing the tobacco sales tax.[148]

The biggest blunder of Jindal's first year came in June when state legislators voted to triple their salaries. Jindal strongly disagreed with the "over the top" pay increases, but said he would not veto the bill.[149] Public outcry was immediate. The legislators backed down slightly and voted to only *double* their salaries, but Louisianans remained incensed.[150] Jindal said "I'm very sorry to see the Legislature do this... More than doubling legislative pay is not reasonable." But, he continued, "I will keep my pledge to let them govern themselves and make their own decisions as a separate branch of government." He vowed not to veto the pay raises.[151]

Anger toward the legislators was soon directed toward Jindal as well. A Baton Rouge resident wrote "I am shocked at Gov. Jindal's refusal to veto the excessive pay-raise bill approved for themselves by the Legislature. This sleazy legislation was ramrodded through when lawmakers knew that voters and constituents were screaming in protest."[152] A Lafayette resident said "I would think a lot more of him and feel that I made the right choice in supporting him if he would veto it." Former State Representative Raymond Lalonde said "I did support him and I'm very disappointed in the leadership he has provided, especially on this issue... To say 'I can't get involved in legislative matters' is a cop-out."[153]

Public outrage soon changed Jindal's mind. He announced on July 1, about a month after the incident began, that he would veto the pay raises. Residents called it "wonderful," "the right decision," and "the best thing he can do," though one added he "should have done it a long time ago."[154] Protestors would have marched at the capital a week later if Jindal had not agreed to the veto. He explained that he "realized this pay raise [was] inconsistent with a new Louisiana." Jindal said he had feared lawmakers would no longer cooperate with him if he vetoed the raises, and having done so, he expected them to be "unhappy."[155]

Some suggested the pay raise debacle was planned by Jindal from the beginning. They speculated Jindal had allowed the legislation to proceed so that Louisianans could see which lawmakers were corrupt. Kenneth Wilks of Baton Rouge wrote,

> I think the veto was planned all along.
>
> This was just the piece of legislation Gov. Bobby Jindal needed to open the eyes of Louisiana residents.

It's a perfect setup. Tell the legislators they can have the raise if they are willing to vote for it, and then once the votes have been cast and there is a record of it, cut their legs out from under them by vetoing the bill.

The plan is elegant in its simplicity.[156]

Whether the pay raise incident was a political maneuver by the governor or just a political misstep, his stalled response seriously jeopardized his public image. Jindal had achieved tremendous popularity and received accolades for his initial ethics reform. Allowing the pay raises would have undermined his ethics legislation and hampered any future efforts for reelection.

Jindal recovered from the incident by toughening the state's sex offender legislation. He signed into law a series of bills that provided harsher penalties for those who harmed minors. The laws included lifetime registration of sex offenders, increased minimum sentences for those who solicit minors or molest juveniles, and provisions for the chemical castration of sex offenders. Jindal told reporters, "We want to let the country know that we'll do everything we can to protect our children… My message to those monsters is, 'You don't want to come to Louisiana.' We are going to protect

50

children from the monsters who would rob their innocence."[157]

Jindal upheld his pledge to fight earmarks. He stripped nearly $16 million in pet projects from the 2008 budget sent to him by lawmakers. The 250 line-item vetoes cut funding for projects like a balloon festival, playground equipment, museums, and the Girl Scouts and Boy Scouts. $39 million in earmarks remained on the budget, but Jindal noted that his vetoes were more than double the line-items vetoed in the previous 12 years combined. Legislators were vocal about their irritation at seeing their projects go.[158]

When Hurricane Gustav hit in September, 2008, Jindal was praised for his effective response. He led orderly evacuations and coordinated with emergency agencies. He purchased $20 million in generators to be sent to local businesses,[159] and then sought to recoup the machines months later when the state had recovered.[160] An op-ed in the Baton Rouge *Advocate* lauded Jindal's performance:

> For the first time in a very long time, we have a governor in whom we can actually take pride - and more so than ever before. During the current hurricane season, Gov. Bobby Jindal has come

forward and proven he is a true leader. His press briefings have been phenomenal. Rather than march a parade of people before the microphones, he demonstrates his grasp of the situation by handling things himself, and does so with unprecedented clarity. You have to listen fast, but the information you need is there.[161]

The global financial crisis hit in September, 2008, shortly after Hurricane Gustav. Louisiana was not immune to the economic downturn. Jindal promised he would not raise taxes to cover the state's budget shortfall. In December he reiterated his desire for reasonable tax and spending decreases: "We would ask the Legislature that they (tax break proposals) would be accompanied with spending cuts."[162] When a massive stimulus bill was passed by Congress in February, 2009, Jindal said he would not have voted for the bill, but would still accept some of the federal funding.[163] He rejected portions that would obligate the state to later raise taxes on businesses.[164]

Jindal continues his first term as governor with a remarkable number of accomplishments already under his belt. He has proven his leadership abilities and maintained a conservative record. At age 37, Jindal's future is wide open. Many conservatives say it is not a question of if, but when, Bobby Jindal will run for president of the United States. Newt Gingrich said in February, 2009, "he will automatically be a major contender for the presidency for many, many years. Remember, he'll be the same age as John McCain 34 years from now. So, he has a long time and he can do a lot of things."[165] If Jindal can maintain his conservative record with integrity, Americans will no doubt continue to look to him for leadership for many years to come.

ACCORDING TO BOBBY JINDAL

Quotes

"I believe in the power of prayer."[166]

"I'm pro-life and I certainly support the traditional definition of marriage."[167]

"We don't need to become liberal to win elections."[168]

"Even when the voters don't agree with you on everything, if they see that you have relevant solutions, they'll support you."[169]

"I think what voters were saying when they elected me [was] 'We're tired of the past. We're tired of corrupt politics. We're tired of the same old politicians. We know we're better than that.'"[170]

"The reality is the Republican Party got itself into trouble. And it got into trouble because the American people didn't see the party offering solutions to the problems they care about" (following Republican losses in the 2008 elections).[171]

"The party's got to do at least three things: number one, we've got to match our actions with our rhetoric. For years we've talked about being the party of low taxes, cutting spending. We went to Washington to change Washington, and we got changed *by* Washington. Number two, we've got to stop defending corruption. We were rightfully criticized in the other party. And finally, number three, we've got to be the party of ideas and solutions... I think there's a path forward for the party, we've just got to be consistent with our principles and stop making excuses for corruption and wasteful spending" (following Republican losses in the 2008 elections).[172]

"It's not going to be enough to simply say 'no' to the Democrats in Washington. We have to show that the conservative principles work."[173]

"If there's any crime other than the taking of a human life that merits the death penalty, that screams out for the death penalty, it's those criminals that harm our children... To me, these are exactly the kinds of crimes that merit the death penalty" (denouncing the Supreme Court's decision outlawing the death penalty for child rapists and defending his authorization of the chemical castration of sex offenders).[174]

"I think Rush [Limbaugh] is a leader for many conservatives and says things that people are concerned about; [he] articulates very well the concern people have about growing government spending without an end in sight."[175]

Speeches

Governor Jindal's victory speech, October 20, 2007:

"Four years ago, I had the privilege of coming and telling you that LSU had beaten Alabama, but that we had lost. Four years later, I'm here to tell you we just took the lead over Auburn -- and we've won.

"Thank you. Thank you. Thank you, Louisiana. Folks, I've got an idea. Let's give our homeland, the great state of Louisiana, a fresh start.

"I want to thank Mr. Campbell, Mr. Boasso, Mr. Georges, the other candidates that offered themselves. This is democracy. Let's give them a round of applause for offering themselves for Louisiana. I also spent some time talking today to Governor Blanco. I'm confident we're going to have a smooth transition. I also want to start – Let's give her a round of applause as well, absolutely.

"I want to start by thanking my wife, my best friend, Supriya. Those who know me well realize there's no Bobby without Supriya. We celebrated our 10th wedding anniversary two nights ago in that most romantic of places, the final debate. I love you, honey. See folks? I really do have a heart after all.

"I also want to thank – You can see them down here – I want to thank our wonderful kids, Selia, Shaan; Slade's actually already in bed right now. They've made a habit – You can see right now – They make a habit of crashing press conferences, disrupting events. I think you're going to get to know them all just a little bit better. I suspect the Governor's mansion's about to become a little bit of a playground. I promise you this: We won't let them color on the walls; don't worry.

"I stand here tonight very humbled by your support. It's hard to describe, but I really feel a heavy sense not only of gratitude to all of you, but of responsibility. More than anything, I stand here tonight tremendously excited and exceedingly optimistic about the opportunity to make real change and to turn our state around.

"You can never adequately thank everybody, but since I do respect my elders, I want to take just a moment to thank my parents. My Mom and Dad came to this country in pursuit of the American Dream. And guess what happened? They found the American Dream to be alive and well right here in Louisiana. They originally chose Louisiana so that my Mom could study at LSU. By the way, go Tigers. Let's beat Auburn tonight. My Dad was the first and only child of nine to even go to high school. Like most of you, my parents walked a much harder road than I've ever walked. I want to thank them publicly for their sacrifices for me and for my brother. But let me say this: My parents have seen what I have seen, that in America and here in Louisiana the only barrier to success is your willingness to work hard and play by the rules.

"Don't let anyone tell you differently. Don't let anyone talk badly about Louisiana. Those days are officially over.

We're serving notice: Louisiana is very soon going to be on the rise. And in recent months many in our nation have gotten the wrong view of Louisiana. A false picture of our state has been painted in many instances. Our state's been depicted as a haven for incompetence and corruption.

"Well, we have some of that, just like every other state does. But let me paint for you the real picture of Louisiana. Here's what I've found while visiting with folks in all 64 parishes and every nook and cranny of our state. The people of Louisiana are God-fearing, hard-working, law-abiding, freedom-loving folks who look out for each other. The people of Louisiana are the salt of the earth.

"They've been so good and kind and generous to my family and me. Look, I was born and raised right here in Baton Rouge. But during this campaign I've seen places in Louisiana that you probably couldn't even find on a map. I've been to many of these places multiple times. I spent so much time in North Louisiana, one of the mayors actually made me an honorary citizen. Five minutes later the local tax assessor gave me a bill.

"There is a ton of work to be done in Baton Rouge. I will devote myself to it fully. But also know this: I'm going to be a Governor who travels the state relentlessly. One thing I know for sure, you can get a distorted view sitting in the halls of government. Things start to look different. The lobbyists begin to look larger and the people begin to look smaller. Reality becomes distorted. I've seen it in Congress as well. I'm not going to let that happen to me. I'm not going to be taken captive by the government crowd in Baton Rouge.

"Today, we begin a new chapter in the history of Louisiana. I've said throughout the campaign that there are two entities that have the most to fear from us winning this election: one is corruption and the other is incompetence. If you happen to see either of them, let them know the party is over.

"I don't want to mislead anyone: This ain't going to be easy. I can't do this by myself. While I can't do it alone, together we can do anything that we set our minds to. Now I know some of you were looking for a little bit of time off, but in many ways our battle has just begun. I suspect that some of those who oppose making big changes in Louisiana government will try to mount a counter-offensive. And some who've been feeding at the trough may not go quietly, but that is up to them. They can either go quietly or they can go loudly, but either way they will go.

"Starting today, every citizen of Louisiana has equal access to state government. Who you know will no longer be more important than what you know. But before we can change the direction of our state, we all have to change our current mindset. We have to defeat cynicism. We have to stop saying 'Oh, politics is always corrupt; there's nothing we can do to straighten out that mess in Baton Rouge.' Sadly, those words roll right off the tongue. We've all become accustomed to thinking that we really can't do anything about the corruption and incompetence in state government.

"We just can't think that way anymore. I'm asking you to believe that we can turn our state around. I'm asking you to give Louisiana another chance. I'm asking you to believe in the greatness of our people. I'm not just asking you to give me a chance, I'm asking you to give yourself a chance. I'm asking you to give us a chance. I'm asking you once again to believe in Louisiana.

"This won't happen overnight. I certainly can't promise you that you'll never again see incompetence or corruption in Louisiana. But I can promise you this: When they rear their heads, they will not be tolerated; no excuses will be accepted. I also can't promise you that I won't make any mistakes. In fact, as Supriya can testify, I can pretty much promise you that I will. But I can also promise you this: When I make mistakes, I'll own up to them; I'll learn from them; I won't be afraid to change course.

"As I promised in the campaign, right after I'm sworn in, I'm going to notify the legislature that I'll be calling them in for a special session to pass real ethics reform with real teeth. It is my intention to work closely with the legislature, and I'm looking forward to it. But please understand this: I'm not going to take 'no' for an answer on reforming our ethics laws. Real ethics reform is not simply campaign rhetoric. It is the lynchpin for change, for regaining the confidence of the voters, for turning our state around. If and when folks try to stop it, I will call them out. If and when people try to throw in amendments designed to derail ethics reform, I will call them out.

"And I'm going to need your help. Ethics reform is the first step in winning the public trust. It is the first step to unlocking our future. It is the first step to growing our economy and bringing great jobs to Louisiana. Before we can create real economic growth, we must show the voters and the entire country that we are serious about changing our reputation. We can do it. We must do it.

"Now look, I do have a major announcement to make: The campaign is over. Now it is time for a fresh start. At times it was a rough campaign. There were a lot of charges and counter-charges thrown out there. It's over. I bear no ill will to anyone. To all those out there who didn't vote for me tonight, I'm asking for your support as well. This campaign is now in the past. I'm not interested in fixing anything in the past. As of this moment, I'm only looking at the future.

"This is a time for us to pull together. Republicans, Democrats, Independents – we're all Louisianians[1] first. North or South – we're all Louisianians first. Rural, suburban, small town, big city – we're all Louisianians first. The time for partisan politics is behind us. This is not my victory tonight. This is our victory tonight.

"The people of Louisiana have spoken, and they've spoken very loudly. They're ready for a fresh start. There's never been before a clearer mandate for change in our state. This is our time. Many have said that the eyes of the nation will be on us. And while that's true, and that's nice to know, that's not what motivates us. Our motivation is pride in our state, pride in our homeland. Our motivation is building great jobs and careers for our kids and for their kids. Our motivation is the firm and unyielding belief that Louisiana can be the greatest place in the world to not only chase the American Dream, but in fact to actually catch it.

"I want to thank God for the many blessings He's bestowed upon me and on all of us. And I want to serve notice on the rest of the country: Keep your eyes on Louisiana. Everyone in the country has helped us in our time of need, and we are very grateful, and we still need help. But please know this: We're simply not going to just try to rebuild. We'll have no part of such a small goal. We're setting our sights much higher. We're getting ready to take off in Louisiana.

"Just like all Americans, you can't keep us down. From our schools, which have failed too many children for too long: We can change. We must change. We will change.

"To our government, which has been too corrupt: We can change. We must change. We will change.

"And our business climate, which has been too weak: We can change. We must change. We will change.

"This state wants change, and I've got one more message tonight: If you're a business looking at expansion, and especially if you're a young person trying to decide where you will make your home, change is not just on the way: Change begins tonight!

"Good night, and may God richly bless you. God bless you."[176]

Governor Jindal's nationally televised response to Barack Obama's first State of the Union Address, February 24, 2009:

"Good evening. I'm Bobby Jindal, Governor of Louisiana.

"Tonight, we witnessed a great moment in the history of our Republic. In the very chamber where Congress once voted to abolish slavery, our first African-American President stepped forward to address the state of our union. With his speech tonight, the President completed a redemptive journey that took our nation from Independence Hall ... to Gettysburg ... to the lunch counter ... and now, finally, the Oval Office.

"Regardless of party, all Americans are moved by the President's personal story - the son of an American mother and a Kenyan father, who grew up to become leader of the free world. Like the President's father, my parents came to this country from a distant land. When they arrived in Baton Rouge, my mother was already 4 ½ months pregnant. I was what folks in the insurance industry now call a "pre-existing condition." To find work, my dad picked up the yellow pages and started calling local businesses. Even after landing a job, he could still not afford to pay for my delivery - so he worked out an installment plan with the doctor. Fortunately for me, he never missed a payment.

"As I grew up, my mom and dad taught me the values that attracted them to this country - and they instilled in me an immigrant's wonder at the greatness of America. As a child, I remember going to the grocery store with my dad. Growing up in India, he had seen extreme poverty. And as we walked through the aisles, looking at the endless variety on the shelves, he would tell me: "Bobby, Americans can do anything." I still believe that to this day. Americans can do anything. When we pull together, there is no challenge we cannot overcome.

"As the President made clear this evening, we are now in a time of challenge. Many of you listening tonight have lost jobs. Others have seen your college and retirement savings dwindle. Many of you are worried about losing your health care and your homes. And you are looking to your elected leaders in Washington for solutions.

"Republicans are ready to work with the new President to provide those solutions. Here in my state of Louisiana, we don't care what party you belong to if you have good ideas to make life better for our people. We need more of that attitude from both Democrats and Republicans in our nation's capital. All of us want our economy to recover and our nation to prosper. So where we agree,

Republicans must be the President's strongest partners. And where we disagree, Republicans have a responsibility to be candid and offer better ideas for a path forward.

"Today in Washington, some are promising that government will rescue us from the economic storms raging all around us.

"Those of us who lived through Hurricane Katrina, we have our doubts.

"Let me tell you a story.

"During Katrina, I visited Sheriff Harry Lee, a Democrat and a good friend of mine. When I walked into his makeshift office I'd never seen him so angry. He was yelling into the phone: "Well, I'm the Sheriff and if you don't like it you can come and arrest me!" I asked him: "Sheriff, what's got you so mad?" He told me that he had put out a call for volunteers to come with their boats to rescue people who were trapped on their rooftops by the floodwaters. The boats were all lined up ready to go - when some bureaucrat showed up and told them they couldn't go out on the water unless they had proof of insurance and registration. I told him, "Sheriff, that's ridiculous." And before I knew it, he was yelling into the phone: "Congressman Jindal is here, and he says you can come and arrest him too!" Harry just told the boaters to ignore the bureaucrats and start rescuing people.

"There is a lesson in this experience: The strength of America is not found in our government. It is found in the compassionate hearts and enterprising spirit of our citizens. We are grateful for the support we have received from across the nation for the ongoing recovery efforts. This spirit got Louisiana through the hurricanes - and this spirit will get our nation through the storms we face today.

"To solve our current problems, Washington must lead. But the way to lead is not to raise taxes and put more money and power in hands of Washington politicians. The way to lead is by empowering you - the American people. Because we believe that Americans can do anything.

"That is why Republicans put forward plans to create jobs by lowering income tax rates for working families … cutting taxes for small businesses … strengthening incentives for businesses to invest in new equipment and

69

hire new workers ... and stabilizing home values by creating a new tax credit for home-buyers. These plans would cost less and create more jobs.

"But Democratic leaders in Congress rejected this approach. Instead of trusting us to make wise decisions with our own money, they passed the largest government spending bill in history - with a price tag of more than $1 trillion with interest. While some of the projects in the bill make sense, their legislation is larded with wasteful spending. It includes $300 million to buy new cars for the government, $8 billion for high-speed rail projects, such as a "magnetic levitation" line from Las Vegas to Disneyland, and $140 million for something called "volcano monitoring." Instead of monitoring volcanoes, what Congress should be monitoring is the eruption of spending in Washington, DC.

"Democratic leaders say their legislation will grow the economy. What it will do is grow the government, increase our taxes down the line, and saddle future generations with debt. Who among us would ask our children for a loan, so we could spend money we do not have, on things we do not need? That is precisely what the Democrats in Congress just did. It's irresponsible.

And it's no way to strengthen our economy, create jobs, or build a prosperous future for our children.

"In Louisiana, we took a different approach. Since I became governor, we cut more than 250 earmarks from our state budget. And to create jobs for our citizens, we cut taxes six times - including the largest income tax cut in the history of our state. We passed those tax cuts with bipartisan majorities. Republicans and Democrats put aside their differences, and worked together to make sure our people could keep more of what they earn. If it can be done in Baton Rouge, surely it can be done in Washington, DC.

"To strengthen our economy, we need urgent action to keep energy prices down. All of us remember what it felt like to pay $4 at the pump - and unless we act now, those prices will return. To stop that from happening, we need to increase conservation ... increase energy efficiency ... increase the use of alternative and renewable fuels ... increase our use of nuclear power - and increase drilling for oil and gas here at home. We believe that Americans can do anything - and if we unleash the innovative spirit of our citizens, we can achieve energy independence.

"To strengthen our economy, we also need to address the crisis in health care. Republicans believe in a simple principle: No American should have to worry about losing their health coverage - period. We stand for universal access to affordable health care coverage. We oppose universal government-run health care. Health care decisions should be made by doctors and patients - not by government bureaucrats. We believe Americans can do anything - and if we put aside partisan politics and work together, we can make our system of private medicine affordable and accessible for every one of our citizens.

"To strengthen our economy, we also need to make sure every child in America gets the best possible education. After Katrina, we reinvented the New Orleans school system - opening dozens of new charter schools, and creating a new scholarship program that is giving parents the chance to send their children to private or parochial schools of their choice. We believe that, with the proper education, the children of America can do anything. And it should not take a devastating storm to bring this kind of innovation to education in our country.

"To strengthen our economy, we must promote confidence in America by ensuring ours is the most ethical and transparent system in the world. In my home state, there used to be saying: At any given time, half of Louisiana is under water - and the other half is under indictment. No one says that anymore. Last year, we passed some of the strongest ethics laws in the nation - and today, Louisiana has turned her back on the corruption of the past. We need to bring transparency to Washington, DC - so we can rid our Capitol of corruption … and ensure we never see the passage of another trillion dollar spending bill that Congress has not even read and the American people haven't even seen.

"As we take these steps, we must remember for all our troubles at home, dangerous enemies still seek our destruction. Now is no time to dismantle the defenses that have protected this country for hundreds of years, or make deep cuts in funding for our troops. America's fighting men and women can do anything. And if we give them the resources they need, they will stay on the offensive … defeat our enemies … and protect us from harm.

"In all these areas, Republicans want to work with President Obama. We appreciate his message of hope - but sometimes it seems we look for hope in different places. Democratic leaders in Washington place their hope in the federal government. We place our hope in you - the American people. In the end, it comes down to an honest and fundamental disagreement about the proper role of government. We oppose the National Democrats' view that says -- the way to strengthen our country is to increase dependence on government. We believe the way to strengthen our country is to restrain spending in Washington, and empower individuals and small businesses to grow our economy and create jobs.

"In recent years, these distinctions in philosophy became less clear - because our party got away from its principles. You elected Republicans to champion limited government, fiscal discipline, and personal responsibility. Instead, Republicans went along with earmarks and big government spending in Washington. Republicans lost your trust - and rightly so.

"Tonight, on behalf of our leaders in Congress and my fellow Republican governors, I say: Our party is determined to regain your trust. We will do so by standing up for the principles that we share ... the principles you elected us to fight for ... the principles that built this into the greatest, most prosperous country on earth.

"A few weeks ago, the President warned that our nation is facing a crisis that he said "we may not be able to reverse." Our troubles are real, to be sure. But don't let anyone tell you that we cannot recover - or that America's best days are behind her. This is the nation that cast off the scourge of slavery ... overcame the Great Depression ... prevailed in two World Wars ... won the struggle for civil rights ... defeated the Soviet menace ... and responded with determined courage to the attacks of September 11, 2001. The American spirit has triumphed over almost every form of adversity known to man - and the American spirit will triumph again.

"We can have confidence in our future - because, amid today's challenges, we also count many blessings: We have the most innovative citizens ...the most abundant resources ... the most resilient economy ... the most powerful military ... and the freest political system in the history of the world. My fellow citizens, never forget: We are Americans. And like my dad said years ago, Americans can do anything.

"Thank you for listening. God bless you. And God bless America."[177]

PHOTOS

Governor Jindal, with his wife Supriya holding the family Bible, takes the Oath of Office from Louisiana Supreme Court Justice Pascal Calogero.

Governor Jindal and the First Lady enter the House Chamber prior to addressing the Legislature. Photo Courtesy of House of Representatives Office of Public Information.

President George W. Bush is greeted by Governor Jindal and his wife, Supriya, on his arrival to Louis Armstrong New Orleans International Airport Monday, April 21, 2008, where President Bush attended the 2008 North American Leaders' Summit. White House photo by Joyce N. Boghosian.

Governor Bobby Jindal speaks to Homeland Security Secretary Michael Chertoff on the tarmac of the New Orleans Lakefront Airport. Photo by La. Department of Transportation and Development.

Governor Jindal and John McCain tour the Ninth Ward after Hurricane Gustav. Photo by Louisiana National Guard.

NOTES

[1] Andrew Romano, "Their Own Obama," *Newsweek*, December 22, 2008.

[2] Rush Limbaugh, "Why We Love Bobby Jindal," *The Rush Limbaugh Show*, EIB Network, February 25, 2009.

[3] Andrew Romano, "Their Own Obama," *Newsweek*, December 22, 2008.

[4] Michelle Malkin, "Even the New York Times thinks Bobby Jindal will win; Update: Victory!" MichelleMalkin.com, October 20, 2007 <http://michellemalkin.com/2007/10/20/even-the-new-york-times-thinks-bobby-jindal-will-win>.

[5] Barack Obama was mocked for his ambiguous former job of "community organizer" in Chicago. See, e.g., "Giuliani's Speech at the Republican National Convention," Election 2008, *The New York Times*, December 1, 2008; also, Jill Lawrence, "'Community organizer' slams attract support for Obama," *USA Today*, September 4, 2008.

[6] Adam Nossiter, "In a Southern U.S. state, immigrants' son takes over," *International Herald Tribune*, October 22, 2007.

[7] "Jindal's ancestral village celebrates his victory," *The Times of India*, October 21, 2007.

[8] Adam Nossiter, "In a Southern U.S. state, immigrants' son takes over," *International Herald Tribune*, October 22, 2007.

[9] "Jindal's ancestral village celebrates his victory," *The Times of India*, October 21, 2007.

[10] Adam Nossiter, "In a Southern U.S. state, immigrants' son takes over," *International Herald Tribune*, October 22, 2007.

[11] "Jindal's success is no surprise to those who know him well," *The Advocate* (Baton Rouge, La.), July 14, 1996.

[12] Andrew Romano, "Their Own Obama," *Newsweek*, December 22, 2008.

[13] Morley Safer, "Bobby Jindal: The GOP's Rising Star?" *60 Minutes*, CBS, March 1, 2009.

[14] "Jindal's success is no surprise to those who know him well," *The Advocate* (Baton Rouge, La.), July 14, 1996.

[15] Morley Safer, "Bobby Jindal: The GOP's Rising Star?" *60 Minutes*, CBS, March 1, 2009.

[16] Andrew Romano, "Their Own Obama," *Newsweek*, December 22, 2008.

[17] Bobby Jindal, "Reflections of a Seven-Year-Old Catholic," *New Oxford Review*, February 1998.

[18] Andrew Romano, "Their Own Obama," *Newsweek*, December 22, 2008.

[19] Andrew Romano, "Their Own Obama," *Newsweek*, December 22, 2008.

[20] Jan Moller, "Anti-Jindal ads provoke religious controversy," *The Times-Picayune*, September 5, 2007.

[21] Jan Moller, "Anti-Jindal ads provoke religious controversy," *The Times-Picayune*, September 5, 2007.

[22] Andrew Romano, "Their Own Obama," *Newsweek*, December 22, 2008.

[23] Andrew Romano, "Their Own Obama," *Newsweek*, December 22, 2008.

[24] Bobby Jindal, "How Catholicism Is Different: The Catholic Church Isn't Just Another Denomination," *New Oxford Review*, April 5, 2006. Available online at freerepublic.com < http://www.freerepublic.com/focus/f-religion/1609536/posts>

[25] Andrew Romano, "Their Own Obama," *Newsweek*, December 22, 2008.

[26] See, e.g., Jan Moller, "Anti-Jindal ads provoke religious controversy," *The Times-Picayune*, September 5, 2007.

[27] Andrew Romano, "Their Own Obama," *Newsweek*, December 22, 2008.

[28] "Jindal's success is no surprise to those who know him well," *The Advocate* (Baton Rouge, La.), July 14, 1996.

[29] "Local teens capture honors at JCL convention," *The Advocate* (Baton Rouge, La.), February 25, 1986.

[30] "BR students take honors at Xavier," *The Advocate* (Baton Rouge, La.), April 11, 1987.

[31] "Beta members conduct state convention," *The Advocate* (Baton Rouge, La.), January 5, 1988.

[32] "State fair winners named," *The Advocate* (Baton Rouge, La.), May 14, 1987.

[33] "Students tour reserve branch," *The Advocate* (Baton Rouge, La.), July 14, 1987.

[34] "Annual scholarship given," *The Advocate* (Baton Rouge, La.), March 24, 1988.

[35] "Jindal's success is no surprise to those who know him well," *The Advocate* (Baton Rouge, La.), July 14, 1996.

[36] Chante Dionne Warren, "Bright Futures *** the Optimist Club of Baton Rouge recognize 10 high school seniors at an awards banquet Nov. 13 for accomplishments in the home, at school, church and in the the community," *The Advocate* (Baton Rouge, La.), November 22, 1997.

[37] "Jindal's success is no surprise to those who know him well," *The Advocate* (Baton Rouge, La.), July 14, 1996.

[38] Andrew Romano, "Their Own Obama," *Newsweek*, December 22, 2008.

[39] Morley Safer, "Bobby Jindal: The GOP's Rising Star?" *60 Minutes*, CBS, March 1, 2009.

[40] Andrew Romano, "Their Own Obama," *Newsweek*, December 22, 2008.

[41] "Junior League of BR celebrates 60th anniversary," *The Advocate* (Baton Rouge, La.), April 5, 1992.

[42] Adam Nossiter, "In a Southern U.S. state, immigrants' son takes over," *International Herald Tribune*, October 22, 2007.

[43] Karen Martin, "New Kid on the Block *** A desire to give something back to the community brought Bobby Jindal home to Louisiana to head up the state Department of Health and Hospitals," *The Advocate* (Baton Rouge, La.), July 14, 1996.

[44] Gerard Shields, "Jindal has big strengths in 1st District," *The Advocate* (Baton Rouge, La.), May 9, 2004.

[45] Karen Martin, "New Kid on the Block *** A desire to give something back to the community brought Bobby Jindal home to Louisiana to head up the state Department of Health and Hospitals," *The Advocate* (Baton Rouge, La.), July 14, 1996.

[46] Andrew Romano, "Their Own Obama," *Newsweek*, December 22, 2008.

[47] Adam Nossiter, "In a Southern U.S. state, immigrants' son takes over," *International Herald Tribune*, October 22, 2007.

[48] "Jindal's success is no surprise to those who know him well," *The Advocate* (Baton Rouge, La.), July 14, 1996.

[49]"DHH pick "Bobby" Jindal young but 'a genius'," *The Advocate* (Baton Rouge, La.), January 6, 1996.

[50] Karen Martin, "New Kid on the Block *** A desire to give something back to the community brought Bobby Jindal home to Louisiana to head up the state Department of Health and Hospitals," *The Advocate* (Baton Rouge, La.), July 14, 1996.

[51] "DHH pick "Bobby" Jindal young but 'a genius'," *The Advocate* (Baton Rouge, La.), January 6, 1996.

[52] Karen Martin, "New Kid on the Block *** A desire to give something back to the community brought Bobby Jindal home to

Louisiana to head up the state Department of Health and Hospitals,"
The Advocate (Baton Rouge, La.), July 14, 1996.

[53] "Jindal's tough stance praised," *The Advocate* (Baton Rouge, La.), February 2, 1996.

[54] Marsha Shuler, "DHH chief vows to recoup overpayments to hospitals," *The Advocate* (Baton Rouge, La.), January 31, 1996.

[55] Marsha Shuler, "State health agency to lay off 185," *The Advocate* (Baton Rouge, La.), March 6, 1996.

[56] Marsha Shuler, "State to add fee for Medicaid," *The Advocate* (Baton Rouge, La.), February 10, 1996.

[57] Marsha Shuler, "Senate panel kills Medicaid co-payment bill," *The Advocate* (Baton Rouge, La.), April 11, 1996.

[58] Bill McMahon, "DHH plans to eliminate program for the needy," *The Advocate* (Baton Rouge, La.), May 10, 1996.

[59] Emily Kern Hebert, "Meet Mrs. Jindal *** Supriya puts promising career on hold for husband, kids," *The Advocate* (Baton Rouge, La.), June 22, 2008.

[60] Scott Dyer, "Jindal vows to battle outmigration," *The Advocate* (Baton Rouge, La.), September 10, 2003.

[61] Emily Kern Hebert, "Meet Mrs. Jindal *** Supriya puts promising career on hold for husband, kids," *The Advocate* (Baton Rouge, La.), June 22, 2008.

[62] Emily Kern Hebert, "Meet Mrs. Jindal *** Supriya puts promising career on hold for husband, kids," *The Advocate* (Baton Rouge, La.), June 22, 2008.

[63] Marsha Shuler, "Jindal leaves DHH to work for Medicare *** Undersecretary Hood named to head agency," *The Advocate* (Baton Rouge, La.), January 29, 1998.

[64] Kristen Lans, "New director of Congressional commission on Medicare reform to speak," The Brown University News Bureau, February 17, 1998

<http://www.brown.edu/Administration/News_Bureau/1997-98/97-084.html>.

[65] Marsha Shuler, "Jindal leaves DHH to work for Medicare *** Undersecretary Hood named to head agency," *The Advocate* (Baton Rouge, La.), January 29, 1998.

[66] "Bobby P. Jindal," National Bipartisan Commission on the Future of Medicare," March 27, 2009 <http://medicare.commission.gov/medicare/jindal_bio.html>.

[67] The "Talking Points" of the National Bipartisan Commission on the Future of Medicare proposal are available online at thomas.loc.gov <http://thomas.loc.gov/medicare/talking.htm>. The text of the proposal is available at medicare.commission.gov <http://medicare.commission.gov/medicare/bbmtt31599.html>.

[68] Sophia McKenzie, "Jindal confident of Medicare plan," *Alexandria Daily Town Talk* (LA), April 6, 1999.

[69] Jim Leggett, "Whiz-kid Bobby Jindal wants to aid La. again," *Alexandria Daily Town Talk* (LA), April 12, 1999.

[70] "Jindal to ask Foster if any jobs available," *The Advocate* (Baton Rouge, La.), March 18, 1999.

[71] Staff, "Jindal will look for big tobacco windfall," *Alexandria Daily Town Talk* (LA), April 18, 1999.

[72] Marsha Shuler, "Jindal is Foster's choice to head university system," *The Advocate* (Baton Rouge, La.), April 21, 1999.

[73] John Hill, "Governor taps Jindal to lead university system," *The Times* (Shreveport, LA), April 21, 1999.

[74] "An academic for Bobby Jindal," *The Advocate* (Baton Rouge, La.), May 14, 1999.

[75] Monica Carter, "New leader unveils plan for universities," *The Times* (Shreveport, La.), May 26, 1999.

[76] "Jindal's big plans for state colleges," *The Advocate* (Baton Rouge, La.), June 21, 1999.

[77] Marsha Shuler, "State colleges to focus on research," *The Advocate* (Baton Rouge, La.), November 7, 1999.

[78] Marsha Shuler, "La. seeks business partnerships for state colleges," *The Advocate* (Baton Rouge, La.), November 12, 1999.

[79] "Professors going to public schools," *The Advocate* (Baton Rouge, La.), March 31, 2000.

[80] "Colleges help business growth," *The Times* (Shreveport, La.), January 15, 2001.

[81] Joan McKinney and Marsha Shuler, "Jindal chosen for key Medicare role," *The Advocate* (Baton Rouge, La.), March 8, 2001.

[82] Emeri O'Brien, "Jindal stops for goodbye," *The News-Star* (Monroe, La.), March 16, 2001.

[83] John Hill, "Foster protege Jindal to run for governor," *Alexandria Daily Town Talk* (La.), February 27, 2003.

[84] Jim Leggett, "Jindal sure sounds official," *Alexandria Daily Town Talk* (La.), March 2, 2003.

[85] John Hill, "Foster protege Jindal to run for governor," *Alexandria Daily Town Talk* (La.), February 27, 2003.

[86] Leesha Faulkner, "Jindal wants students to stay," *The News Star* (Monroe, La.), March 25, 2003.

[87] Leesha Faulkner, "Jindal wants students to stay," *The News Star* (Monroe, La.), March 25, 2003.

[88] Scott Dyer, "Candidates say bringing jobs to La. will be high priority," *The Advocate* (Baton Rouge, La.), April 8, 2003.

[89] Chris Frink, "Bobby Jindal tells Kiwanians he'll turn Louisiana around," *The Advocate* (Baton Rouge, La.), June 5, 2003.

[90] Adam Nossiter, "Jindal's assets also difficulties as candidate," *The Advocate* (Baton Rouge, La.), April 28, 2003.

[91] Robbie Evans, "Gubernatorial candidates make campaign tour stop," *The News-Star* (Monroe, La.), May 8, 2003.

[92] Christy Futch, "Jindal discusses faith, values," *The News-Star* (Monroe, La.), July 1, 2003.

[93] Mike Hasten, "Candidates split on school voucher issue," *The Daily Advertiser* (Lafayette, La.), March 21, 2003.

[94] Chris Frink, "Bobby Jindal tells Kiwanians he'll turn Louisiana around," *The Advocate* (Baton Rouge, La.), June 5, 2003.

[95] John Hill, "Jindal: First phone will be to Bush," *Alexandria Daily Town Talk* (La.), July 10, 2003.

[96] Brent Tippen, "Jindal offers best choice for governor," Letters to the Editor, *The News-Star* (Monroe, La.), July 3, 2003.

[97] "Politics," *The Advocate* (Baton Rouge, La.), March 30, 2003.

[98] Adam Nossiter, "Jindal's assets also difficulties as candidate," *The Advocate* (Baton Rouge, La.), April 28, 2003.

[99] "Election 2003," *The Daily Advertiser* (Lafayette, La.), October 5, 2003.

[100] Chris Frink, "Buddy Leach endorses Blanco, blasts Jindal in gubernatorial race," *The Advocate* (Baton Rouge, La.), October 10, 2003.

[101] Chris Frink, "La.'s top Democrats back Blanco," *The Advocate* (Baton Rouge, La.), October 11, 2003.

[102] "Politics," *The Advocate* (Baton Rouge, La.), October 12, 2003.

[103] John Hill, "Blanco, Jindal support death penalty," *The Alexandria Daily Town Talk* (La.), November 11, 2003.

[104] Scott Dyer, "Governor candidates differ on abortion but agree on guns, gays," *The Advocate* (Baton Rouge, La.), October 26, 2003.

[105] Mike Hasten, "Jindal gets endorsement of black group," *The Daily Advertiser* (Lafayette, La.), October 24, 2003.

[106] John Hill, "La. elects first woman governor," *The Alexandria Daily Town Talk* (La.), November 16, 2003.

[107] John Hill, "La. elects first woman governor," *The Alexandria Daily Town Talk* (La.), November 16, 2003.

[108] Mike Hasten, "Jindal supporters lost hope as night wore on," *The Daily Advertiser* (Lafayette, La.), November 16, 2003.

[109] Scott Dyer, "Jindal responds to critics, doesn't regret strategy," *The Advocate* (Baton Rouge, La.), November 17, 2003.

[110] Patrick Courreges, "Four congressional races appear settled – two in runoffs," *The Advocate* (Baton Rouge, La.), November 3, 2004.

[111] Gerard Shields, "New La. congressmen catching up fast," *The Advocate* (Baton Rouge, La.), December 19, 2004.

[112] "Jindal already getting profile," *The Advocate* (Baton Rouge, La.), December 14, 2004.

[113] Gerard Shields, "Jindal has big strengths in 1st District," *The Advocate* (Baton Rouge, La.), May 9, 2004.

[114] For a more user-friendly search of Jindal's Congressional voting record, see Project Vote Smart <http://www.votesmart.org>.

[115] S 1701: Extension of Funding for Transitional Medical Assistance and Abstinence Education.

[116] Marsha Shuler and Gerard Shields, "Blanco, Jindal rap Bush SCHIP veto *** Other GOP congressmen back action," *The Advocate* (Baton Rouge, La.), October 4, 2007.

[117] H J Res 27: Withdrawing Approval from the WTO Agreement.

[118] H Con Res 63: Iraq War Policy Resolution

[119] Morley Safer, "Bobby Jindal: The GOP's Rising Star?" *60 Minutes*, CBS, March 1, 2009.

[120] See, e.g., Dan Turner, "Bush's visit highlights need for faster action, less blame," *The Time* (Shreveport, La.), September 6, 2005.

[121] Penny Brown Roberts, "Locals join criticism of tardy response," *The Advocate* (Baton Rouge, La.), September 12, 2005.

[122] Gerard Shields, "Angelle pleads for more funds," *The Advocate* (Baton Rouge, La.), September 12, 2005.

[123] Gerard Shields, "Politicians affected by Katrina," *The Advocate* (Baton Rouge, La.), September 18, 2005.

[124] Penny Brown Roberts, "Locals join criticism of tardy response," *The Advocate* (Baton Rouge, La.), September 12, 2005.

[125] Gerard Shields, "La. lobbies for more disaster aid," *The Advocate* (Baton Rouge, La.), December 12, 2005.

[126] Sheriff Jack A. Stephens, "Opinion: Letters to Editor," *The Daily Advertiser* (Lafayette, La.), March 14, 2006.

[127] Russ Marsh, "Deceptive Democratic spin," *The Alexandria Daily Town Talk* (La.), September 21, 2005.

[128] Michelle Millhollon, "Jindal says he's weighing gubernatorial option," *The Advocate* (Baton Rouge, La.), November 9, 2006.

[129] Michelle Millhollon, "Jindal says he's in the race *** He wants rematch against Blanco," *The Advocate* (Baton Rouge, La.), January 23, 2007.

[130] Robert Morgan, "Candidate Jindal: 'I know we can change our state'," *Alexandria Daily Town Talk* (La.), July 17, 2007.

[131] Greg Hilburn, "Jindal presents 25-point plan for government reform," *The News-Star* (Monroe, La.), August 17, 2007.

[132] Kyle Jackson, "Jindal unveils his economic platform," *The Daily Advertiser* (Lafayette, La.), September 18, 2007.

[133] Michelle Millhollon, "Blanco won't seek re-election *** Governor hopes to check politics," *The Advocate* (Baton Rouge, La.), March 21, 2007.

[134] Tinsley Ducote, "Negative ad a terrible mistake," *Alexandria Daily Town Talk* (La.), September 2, 2007.

[135] Lee Fletcher, "Attack ads misleading," *Alexandria Daily Town Talk* (La.), September 2, 2007.

[136] Will Sentell, "Jindal carries 60 parishes in landslide win," *The Advocate* (Baton Rouge, La.), October 22, 2007.

[137] Michelle Millhollon, "Jindal apparent winner *** Main foes concede election," *The Advocate* (Baton Rouge, La.), October 21, 2007.

[138] "Jindal's ancestral village celebrates his victory," *The Times of India*, October 21, 2007.

[139] Michelle Millhollon, "Jindal freezes government hiring," *The Advocate* (Baton Rouge, La.), January 16, 2008.

[140] "Ethics path to new jobs," *The Advocate* (Baton Rouge, La.), February 13, 2008.

[141] Mike Hasten, "Jindal satisfies premier pledge," *The News-Star* (Monroe, La.), February 27, 2008.

[142] Greg Hilburn, "Jindal hails success of ethics session," *The News-Star* (Monroe, La.), February 28, 2008.

[143] Michelle Millhollon, "Jindal plan: $30 billion *** Official: Budget reflects 12 percent cut," *The Advocate* (Baton Rouge, La.), March 1, 2008.

[144] Michelle Millhollon, "Special session 2 *** Jindal turns eyes to business in sequel," *The Advocate* (Baton Rouge, La.), March 10, 2008.

[145] Greg Hilburn, "Jindal rolls in first 100 days," *The News-Star* (Monroe, La.), April 27, 2008.

[146] "Jindal keeps his promises," *The News-Star* (Monroe, La.), April 28, 2008.

[147] Michelle Millhollon, "Bill to end income tax stalls *** Legislators work on tax-cut proposals," *The Advocate* (Baton Rouge, La.), May 13, 2008.

[148] "Tobacco tax on the rise," *The Advocate* (Baton Rouge, La.), May 28, 2008.

[149] Marsha Shuler, "Jindal won't stop raise *** House pay bill vote due Friday," *The Advocate* (Baton Rouge, La.), June 12, 2008.

[150] Marsha Shuler, "Pay plan cut back *** House OKs bill to double salary instead of tripling it," *The Advocate* (Baton Rouge, La.), June 14, 2008.

[151] Mike Hasten, "Jindal stands by pay raises," *The News-Star* (Monroe, La.), June 17, 2008.

[152] Patrick Stockstill, "Jindal betrayal deeply shocking," Readers' Views, *The Advocate* (Baton Rouge, La.), June 26, 2008.

[153] Claire Taylor, "Supporters question his no-veto decision," *The Daily Advertiser* (Lafayette, La.), June 28, 2008.

[154] "Jindal vetoes pay raise *** 'What do you think about Gov. Bobby Jindal's decision to veto the legislative pay raises?'" *The Advocate* (Baton Rouge, La.), July 1, 2008.

[155] Michelle Millhollon, "Jindal vetoes pay raise *** Governor: Act will miff legislators," *The Advocate* (Baton Rouge, La.), July 1, 2008.

[156] Kenneth Wilks, "Reader says Jindal set up lawmakers," *The Advocate* (Baton Rouge, La.), July 1, 2008.

[157] Greg Hilburn, "Governor to predators: Stay away from La.," *The News-Star* (Monroe, La.), July 3, 2008.

[158] Melinda Deslatte, "Governor smashes $16M in earmarks," *The News-Star* (Monroe, La.), July 15, 2008.

[159] "State to hand out $20M in generators," *The Advocate* (Baton Rouge, La.), September 5, 2008.

[160] Marsha Shuler, "State wants generators used in storm returned," *The Advocate* (Baton Rouge, La.), November 21, 2008.

[161] Stephen Winham, "Jindal proves himself a true leader," *The Advocate* (Baton Rouge, La.), September 19, 2008.

[162] Mark Ballard and Michelle Millhollon, "Tax breaks possible despite shortfall *** Jindal open to tax credits that 'make sense'," *The Advocate* (Baton Rouge, La.), December 19, 2008.

[163] Gerard Shields, "Stimulus plan passes *** Package to bring $3.8 billion to La.," *The Advocate* (Baton Rouge, La.), February 14, 2009.

[164] Michelle Millhollon, "Jindal will take $2 billion in stimulus," *The Advocate* (Baton Rouge, La.), March 5, 2009.

[165] Morley Safer, "Bobby Jindal: The GOP's Rising Star?" *60 Minutes*, CBS, March 1, 2009.

[166] David Dinsmore, "Jindal: 'I believe in the power of prayer'," *Alexandria Daily Town Talk* (La.), July 3, 2008.

[167] "2008 presidential series with Wolf Blitzer," CNN, June 29, 2008.

[168] "The road ahead for the Republican Party," *Hannity & Colmes*, Fox News, November 5, 2008.

[169] Andrew Romano, "Their Own Obama," *Newsweek*, December 22, 2008.

[170] Morley Safer, "Bobby Jindal: The GOP's Rising Star?" *60 Minutes*, CBS, March 1, 2009.

[171] Morley Safer, "Bobby Jindal: The GOP's Rising Star?" *60 Minutes*, CBS, March 1, 2009.

[172] "The road ahead for the Republican Party," *Hannity & Colmes*, Fox News, November 5, 2008.

[173] Interview with Greta Van Susteren, *On the Record*, Fox News, November 12, 2008.

[174] "Governor signs chemical castration bill," *Cavuto*, Fox News, June 26, 2008.

[175] *Larry King Live*, CNN, March 2, 2009.

[176] G. Andrew Boyd, "Bobby Jindal's entire victory speech," news video, *The Times-Picayune*, October 21, 2007 <http://blog.nola.com/tpvideo/2007/10/bobby_jindals_entire_victory_s.html>. Unedited transcript available from American Rhetoric <http://www.americanrhetoric.com/speeches/bobbyjindallouisianago vvictory.htm>.

[177] "Governor Bobby Jindal: 'Americans Can Do Anything'," Louisiana Office of the Governor, February 24, 2009 <http://www.gov.state.la.us/index.cfm?md=newsroom&tmp=detail& catID=3&articleID=1032&navID=11>.

Made in the USA